LET'S PLAY SPORTS!

Archery

by Kieran Downs

BLASTOFF!
2
READERS

BELLWETHER MEDIA • MINNEAPOLIS, MN

Blastoff! Readers are carefully developed by literacy experts to build reading stamina and move students toward fluency by combining standards-based content with developmentally appropriate text.

Level 1 provides the most support through repetition of high-frequency words, light text, predictable sentence patterns, and strong visual support.

Level 2 offers early readers a bit more challenge through varied sentences, increased text load, and text-supportive special features.

Level 3 advances early-fluent readers toward fluency through increased text load, less reliance on photos, advancing concepts, longer sentences, and more complex special features.

★ **Blastoff! Universe**

Reading Level

Grade
K

Grades
1–3

Grade
4

This edition first published in 2021 by Bellwether Media, Inc.

No part of this publication may be reproduced in whole or in part without written permission of the publisher. For information regarding permission, write to Bellwether Media, Inc., Attention: Permissions Department, 6012 Blue Circle Drive, Minnetonka, MN 55343.

Library of Congress Cataloging-in-Publication Data

Names: Downs, Kieran, author.
Title: Archery / by Kieran Downs.
Description: Minneapolis, MN : Bellwether Media Inc., [2021] | Series: Blastoff! Readers: Let's Play Sports! | Includes bibliographical references and index. | Audience: Ages 5-8 | Audience: Grades K-1 | Summary: "Relevant images match informative text in this introduction to archery. Intended for students in kindergarten through third grade"–Provided by publisher.
Identifiers: LCCN 2019053835 (print) | LCCN 2019053836 (ebook) | ISBN 9781644872154 (library binding) | ISBN 9781618919731 (ebook)
Subjects: LCSH: Archery–Juvenile literature.
Classification: LCC GV1189 .D69 2021 (print) | LCC GV1189 (ebook) | DDC 799.3/2–dc23
LC record available at https://lccn.loc.gov/2019053835
LC ebook record available at https://lccn.loc.gov/2019053836

Editor: Christina Leaf   Designer: Josh Brink

Printed in the United States of America, North Mankato, MN.

Table of Contents

What Is Archery?

Archery is one of the oldest sports in the world.

Archers use **bows** and **arrows**. They shoot at **targets** for points.

target

arrows

bow

Archery is popular around the world. South Korea has won many **Olympic** medals in the sport.

- **South Korean National Team**

- **outdoor recurve events**

- **Accomplishments:**
  - **Individual and team gold medals in the 2016 Rio Olympics**
  - **Team silver medal at the 2019 world championships**

Archers compete by themselves or in teams.

What Are the Rules for Archery?

There are two main kinds of archery. Target archery is done on a long **range**.

Archers move around a course in field archery.

field archery

target archery

range

Archers get points based on
how well they shoot.

Range targets usually have rings with many colors. Hitting the **bull's-eye** scores ten points.

ARCHERY RECURVE TARGET

bull's-eye

1 2 3 4 5 6 7 8 9 10 10 10 9 8 7 6 5 4 3 2 1

points

In target archery, archers go **head-to-head**. They shoot three arrows in a **set**.

Whoever shoots the highest score gets two set points. The first to score six set points wins.

Archery can be dangerous. Archers must be careful.

On ranges, everyone shoots together. They collect arrows at the same time, too.

Archery Gear

compound bow

← pulley

There are two kinds of bows. Compound bows are easier to shoot.

They use **pulleys**.
These help archers
pull back the string.

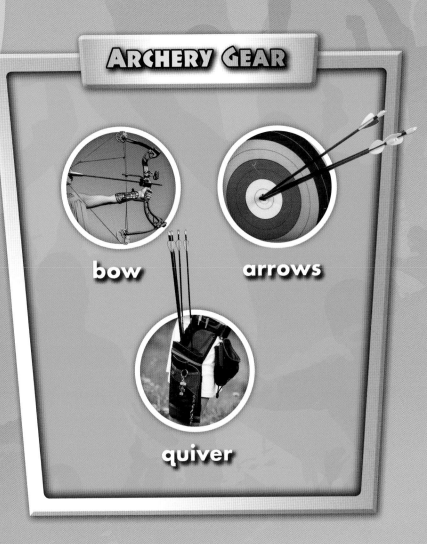

ARCHERY GEAR

bow

arrows

quiver

Recurve bows take more strength. They have three main parts. Archers hold the **grip**. The string is connected to two **limbs**.

limb

grip

recurve bow

Recurve bows are the only
bows used in the Olympics.

Quivers hold arrows. Archers must be able to reach them easily.

Each arrow must be the same size. Aim for the bulls-eye!

quiver

Glossary

arrows—thin, straight tools shot from bows that have a sharpened tip in the front

bows—tools for shooting arrows made from a curved piece of material with its ends joined by a tight string

bull's-eye—the smallest ring in the middle of a target

grip—the part of a recurve bow that holds an arrow in place and that the archer holds onto

head-to-head—when archers face off against one another

limbs—the parts of a recurve bow that connect to the string

Olympic—related to the Olympic Games; the Olympic Games are worldwide summer or winter sports contests held in a different country every four years.

pulleys—simple machines using ropes and wheels that make lifting easier

quivers—cases for holding arrows that can be worn on the body

range—the area in between the archer and the target; archery targets are often placed up to 295 feet (90 meters) away from the archer.

set—a group of games that count towards deciding a winner; archery has up to five sets.

targets—the objects archers shoot at

To Learn More

AT THE LIBRARY

Downs, Kieran. *Fishing*. Minneapolis, Minn.:
Bellwether Media, 2021.

Nayeri, Daniel. *The Most Dangerous Book: An
Illustrated Introduction to Archery*. New York, N.Y.:
Workman Publishing Co., 2017.

Omoth, Tyler. *Bowhunting*. Lake Elmo, Minn.: Focus
Readers, 2018.

ON THE WEB

FACTSURFER

Factsurfer.com gives you
a safe, fun way to find
more information.

1. Go to www.factsurfer.com.

2. Enter "archery" into the search box
   and click Q.

3. Select your book cover to see a list
   of related content.

Index

The images in this book are reproduced through the courtesy of: emholk, front cover (girl), p. 5; Imfoto, front cover (background); kontrymphoto, p. 4; Yves Herman/ Newscom, p. 6; Sam Bryant/ Wikipedia, p. 7; Mr. Barndoor/ Wikipedia, p. 8; CP DC Press, p. 9; CSP_shariffc/ Age Fotostock, p. 10; Alexander Rochau, p. 12; Sergey Ryzhov, p. 13; Jeff Gilbert/ Alamy, p. 14; Chatchai Somwat, p. 15; Shane W Thompson, p. 16; Ben Schonewille, p. 17 (top left); kirilldz, p. 17 (top right); Svetograf, pp. 17 (bottom), 21; Dm_Cherry, p. 18; Nippon News/ Alamy, p. 19; seirceil, p. 20; Hibridia, p. 23.